A NEW N

Written By Carly Menker   Illustrated by Bonnie Lemaire

Copyright © 2016 Carly Menker
All rights reserved.
ISBN: 1535108215
ISBN 13: 978-1535108218

CreateSpace Independent Publishing Platform
North Charleston, South Carolina

To my family, and to anyone out there battling an adversity.
Believe in yourself and you can do it!

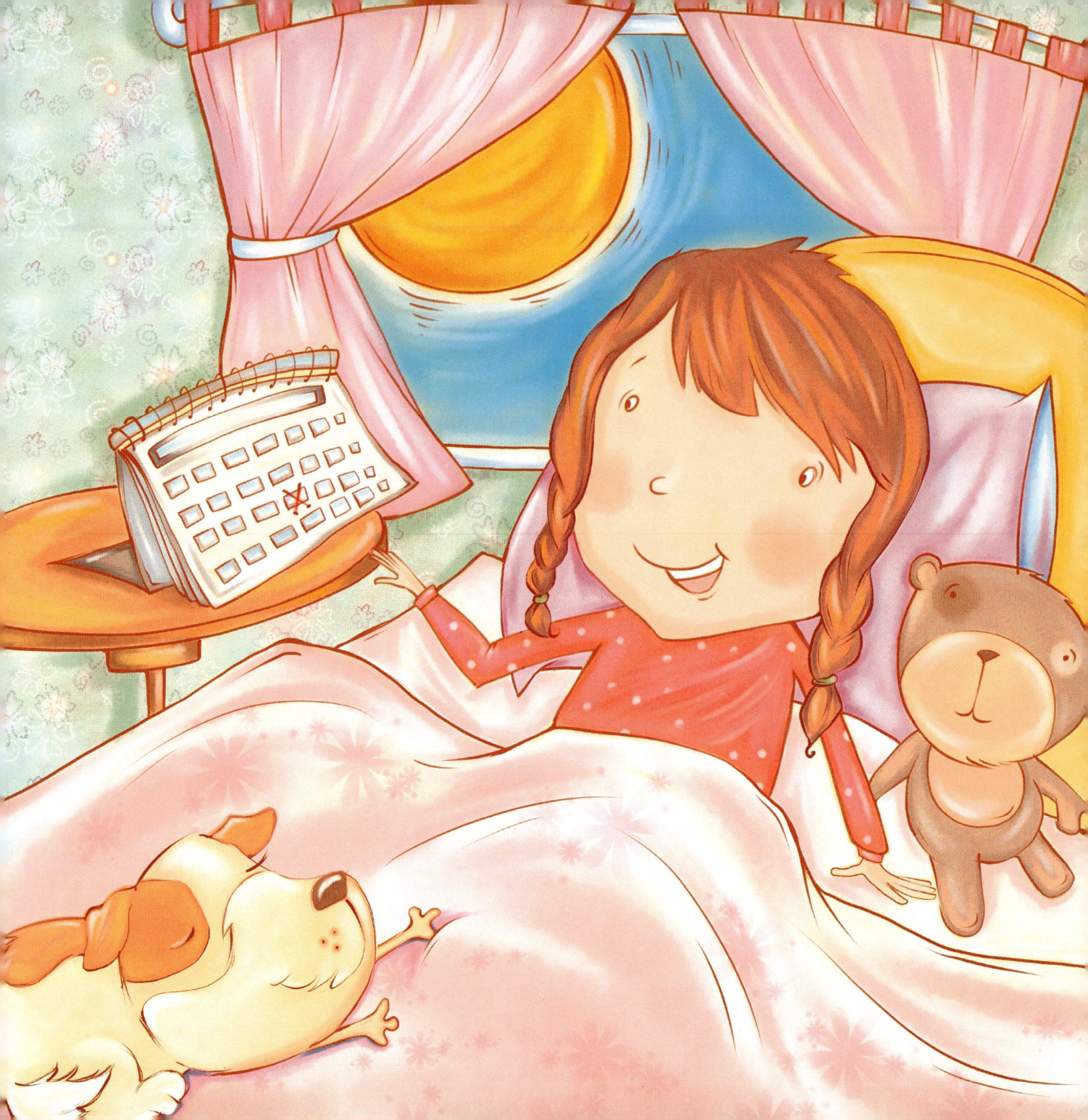

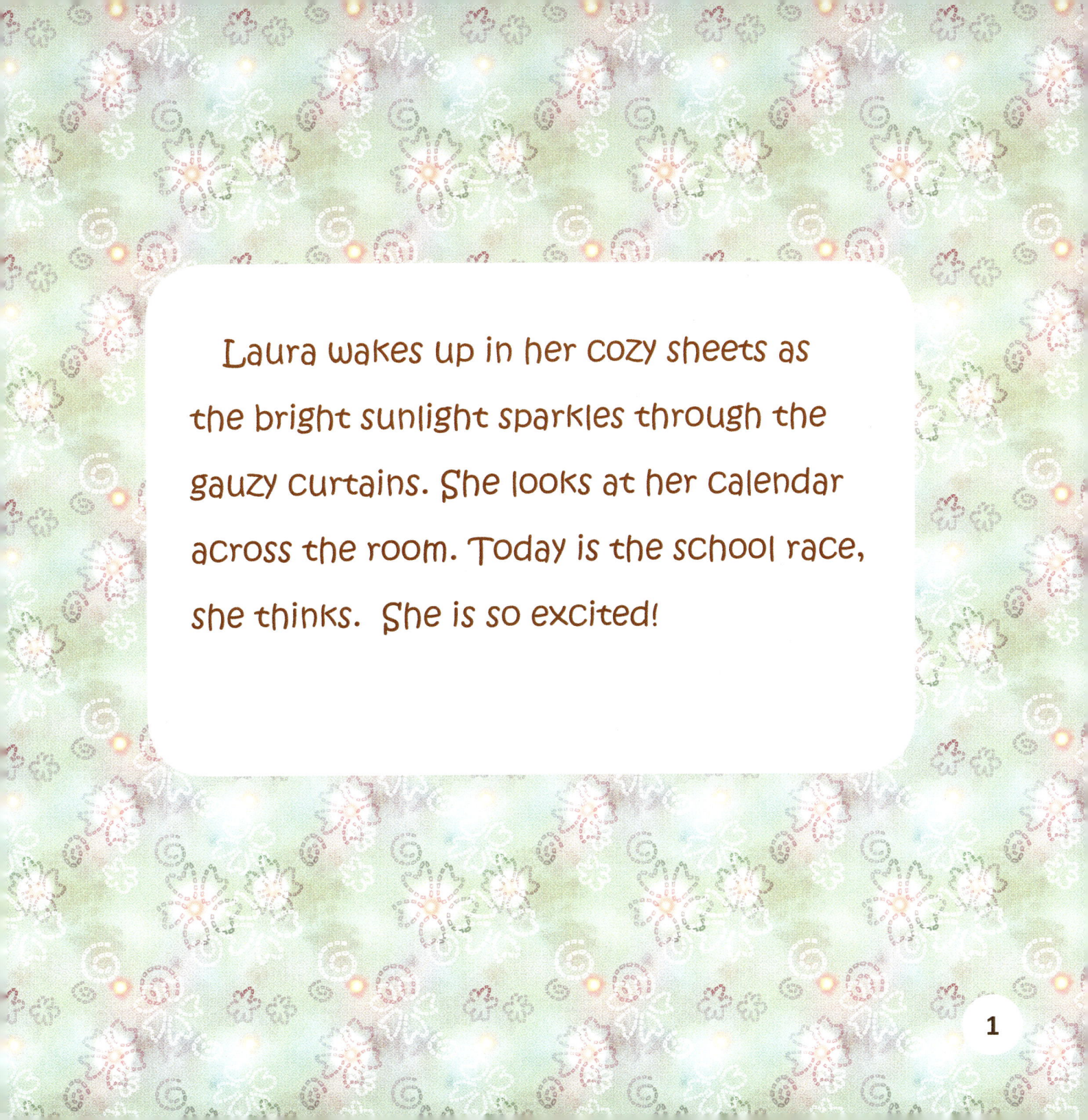

Laura wakes up in her cozy sheets as the bright sunlight sparkles through the gauzy curtains. She looks at her calendar across the room. Today is the school race, she thinks. She is so excited!

2

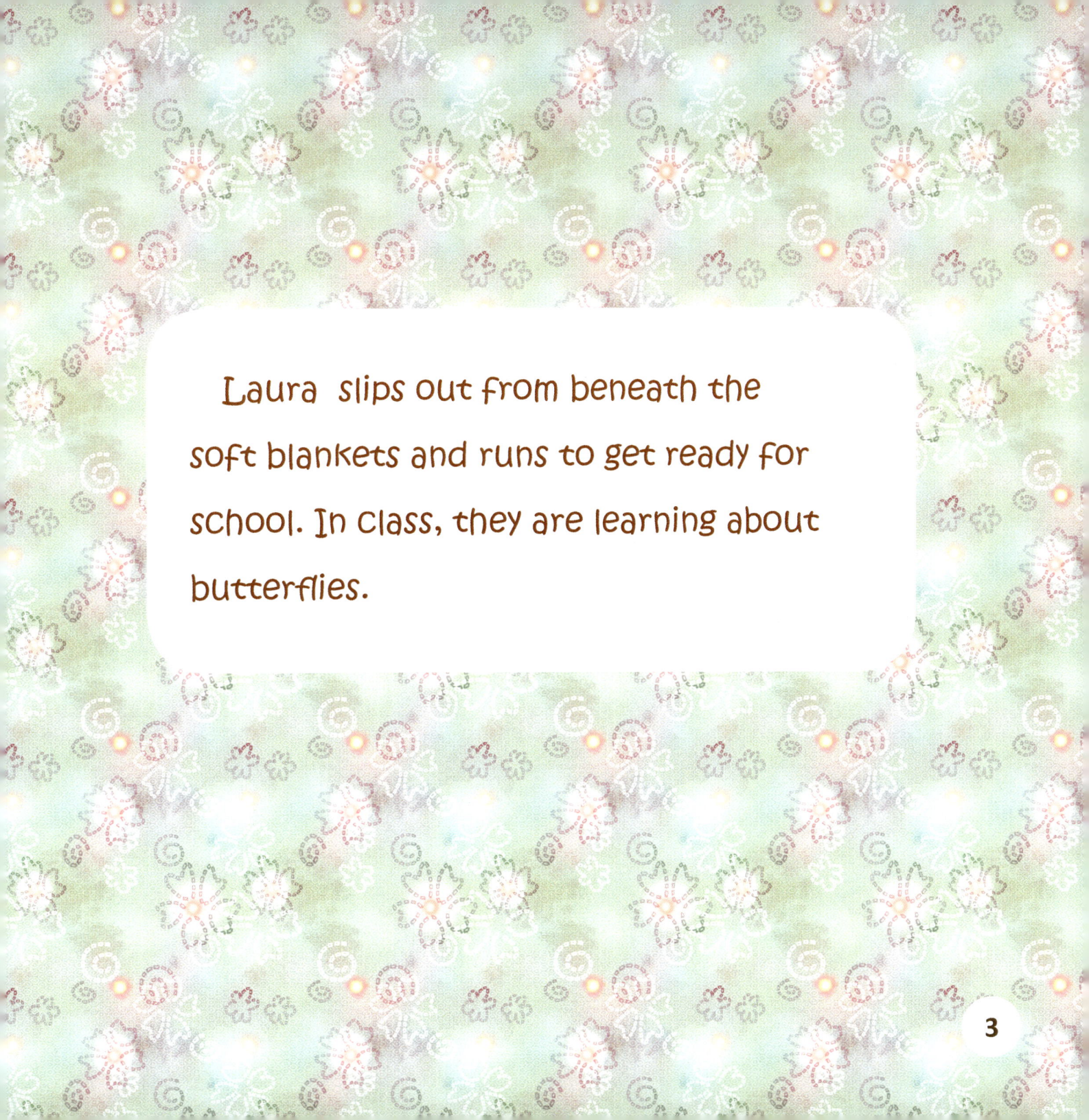

Laura slips out from beneath the soft blankets and runs to get ready for school. In class, they are learning about butterflies.

Racing to catch the bus, Laura grabs her backpack and a very important package wrapped in a napkin. It is her medication.

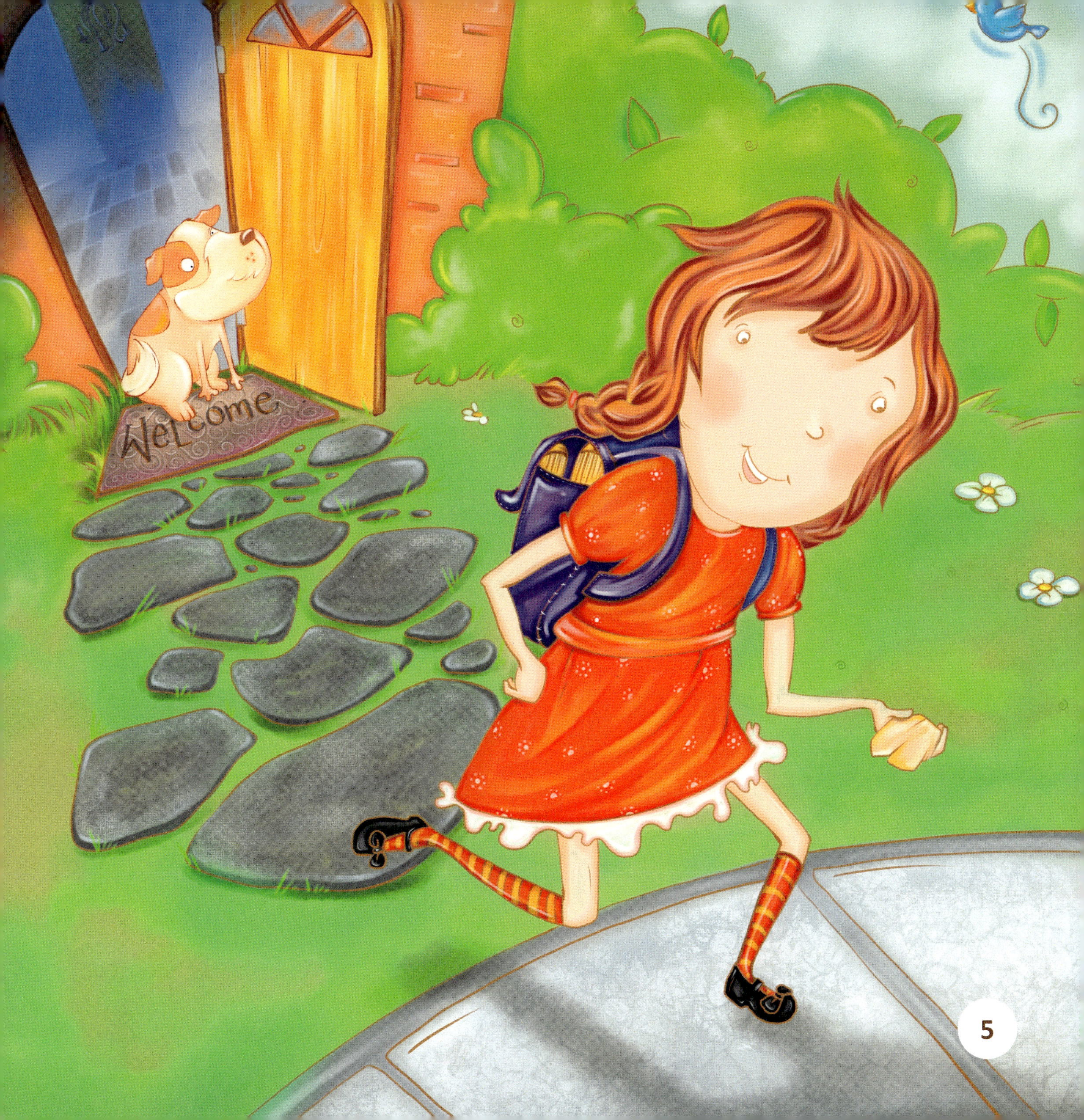
Welcome

As Laura waits at the bench for her bus, she pours the contents of the napkin into her hand. She counts three yellow pills, one blue and one green one, and four white ones. They don't taste too bad, she thinks.

7

She pours them one after another into her mouth, and swallows them with big gulps of water. Her best friend, Sami, walks toward her at the bench.

"What are those?" Sami asks.

9

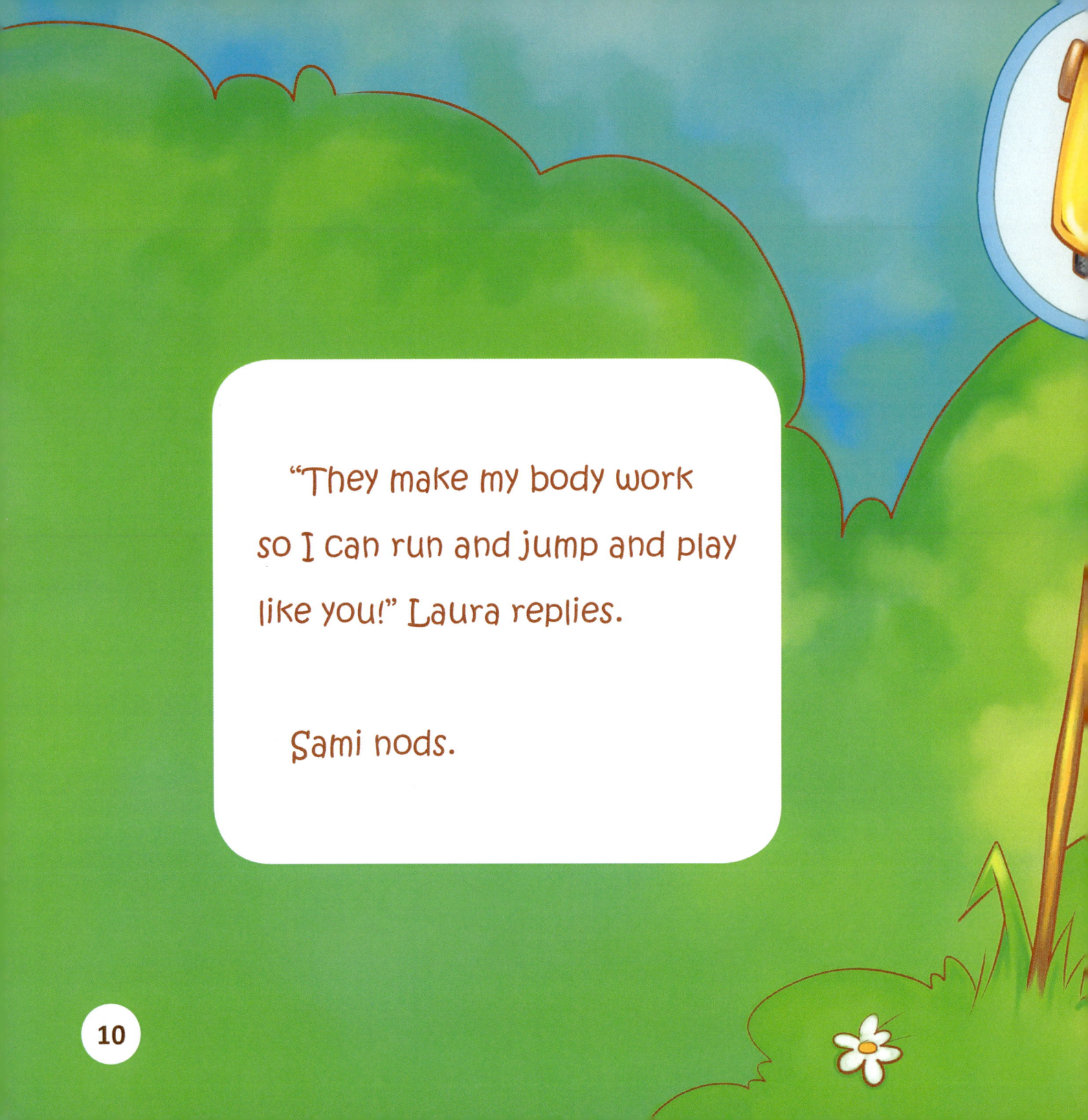

"They make my body work so I can run and jump and play like you!" Laura replies.

Sami nods.

11

Laura and Sami board the bus. Sitting together, Laura wonders what they are going to do in class today. Maybe the class shipment of caterpillars came!

13

Suddenly, Laura begins to feel very sick to her stomach. Oh no. Not again, she thinks. Laura slaps her hand over her mouth and bolts off the bus towards the bathroom at school.

SCHOOL ZONE

Sami waits for Laura in the bathroom. "Wipe the worry off your face. This is normal for me," Laura says to Sami.

17

Washing her hands and no longer queasy, Laura smiles at Sami. "I just have Crohn's disease. It causes my belly to hurt and my body to attack itself. But, I'll be okay. This is my normal. I'm no different from you." Laura says.

"I know. I know. You tell me everyday!" Sami says back.

19

The bell rings and the girls take their seats in class.

"Good morning, everyone," their teacher says. "After lunch we will prepare to clip our caterpillar cocoons in the tanks for our butterflies. They have arrived."

The class erupts in cheers.

21

Laura slips out of her seat and looks up at the teacher from the doorway. She nods, and then rushes to the bathroom.

23

Twenty minutes later, Laura comes back quietly to her seat, careful not to interrupt the teacher's lesson.

"Where were you?" Sami asks in a hushed tone.

"The bathroom. Please stop worrying! It's my normal," Laura says.

25

"She always leaves class SO MUCH!"

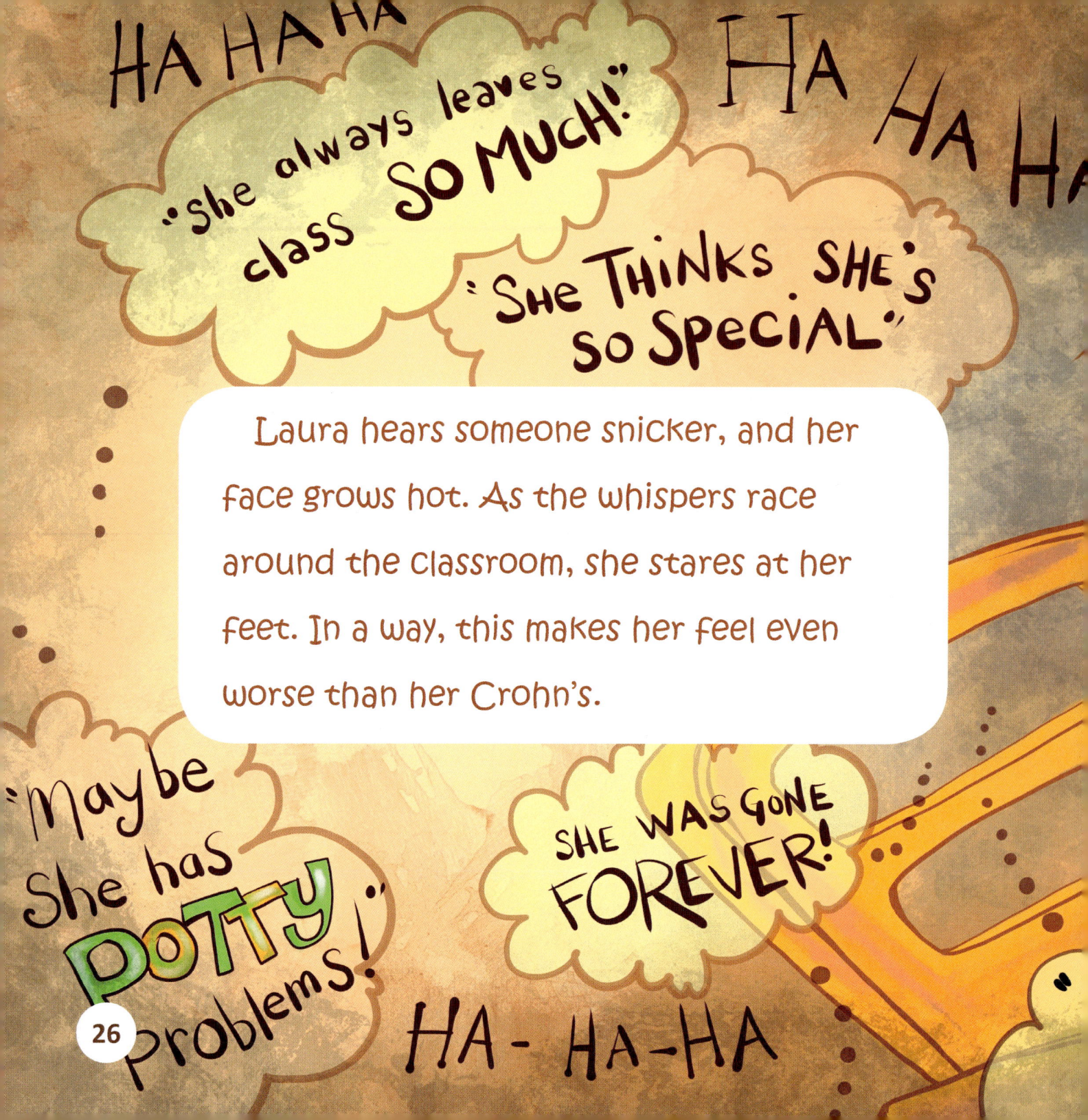

HA HA HA HA HA HA

"SHE THINKS SHE'S SO SPECIAL."

Laura hears someone snicker, and her face grows hot. As the whispers race around the classroom, she stares at her feet. In a way, this makes her feel even worse than her Crohn's.

"Maybe she has POTTY problems!"

"SHE WAS GONE FOREVER!"

HA-HA-HA

"DID YOU SEE LAURA?"

"...s so weird"

"Hey!" Sami snaps back at the whisperers. "Stop being mean. Laura has a medical thing that is not something you need to worry about. Leave her alone."

29

Laura tries to hide her smile and looks at the floor. She can't imagine what she'd do without Sami.

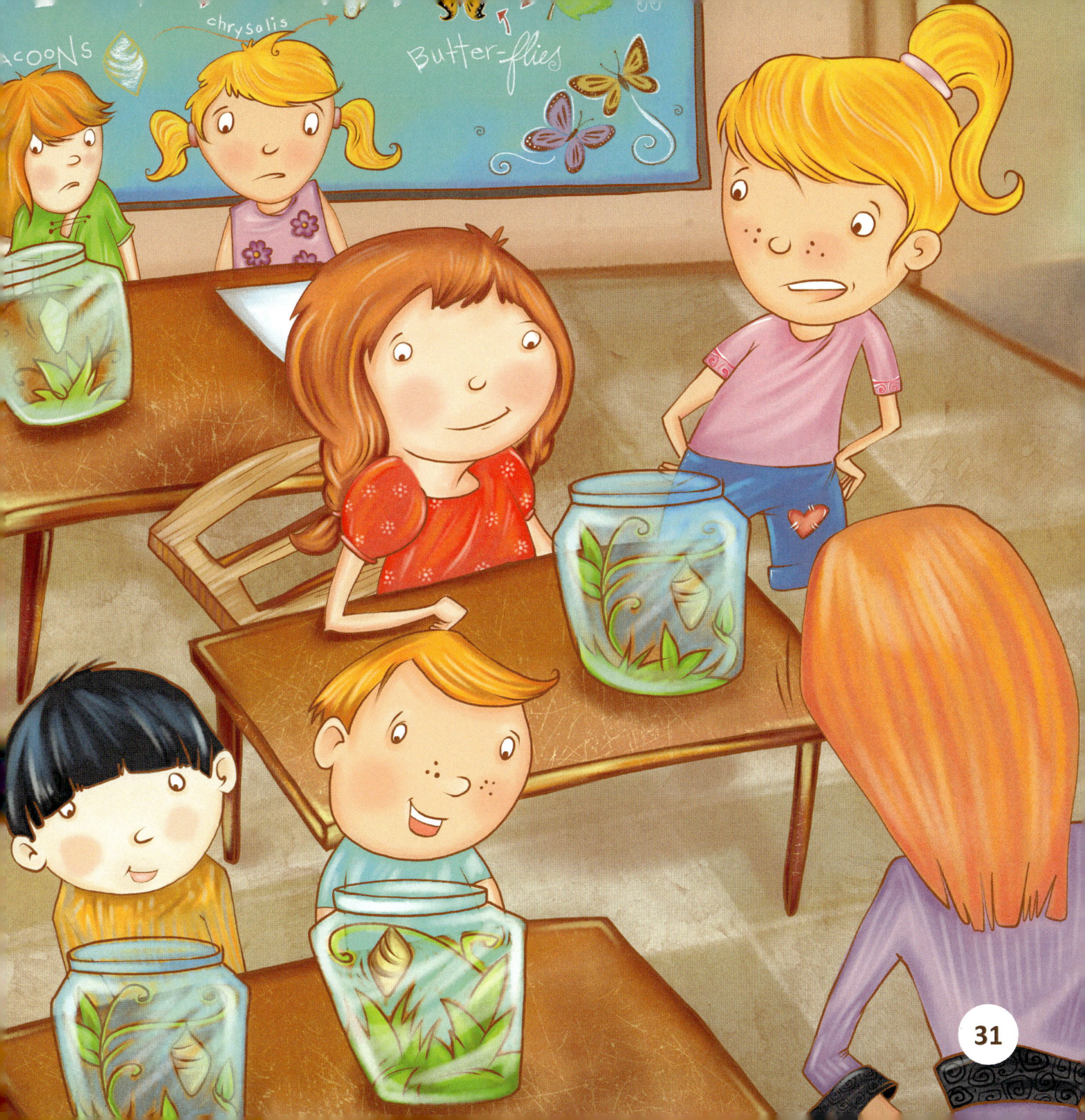
cocoons
chrysalis
Butter-flies

The bell rings again and it's time for lunch. Not everyone who has Crohn's has a special diet, everyone is different, but each person with Crohn's needs to be careful of what they're eating. Laura's Crohn's prevents her from eating gluten, popcorn, raw vegetables, and nuts, so she eats a turkey and cheese rice-cake sandwich almost everyday. Laura loves not having to eat her vegetables as she watches Sami eat the carrots she hates.

33

Laura looks at the clock on the lunchroom wall. It's time for recess, she thinks. The cafeteria teachers begin to motion everyone outside into the open field and playground back behind the school. Today, the fifth graders are having races during recess.

35

It's Laura's turn. She runs as fast as she can, ignoring all of the possible things that could go wrong for her. She keeps running and running, just as good and just as fast as the other kids.

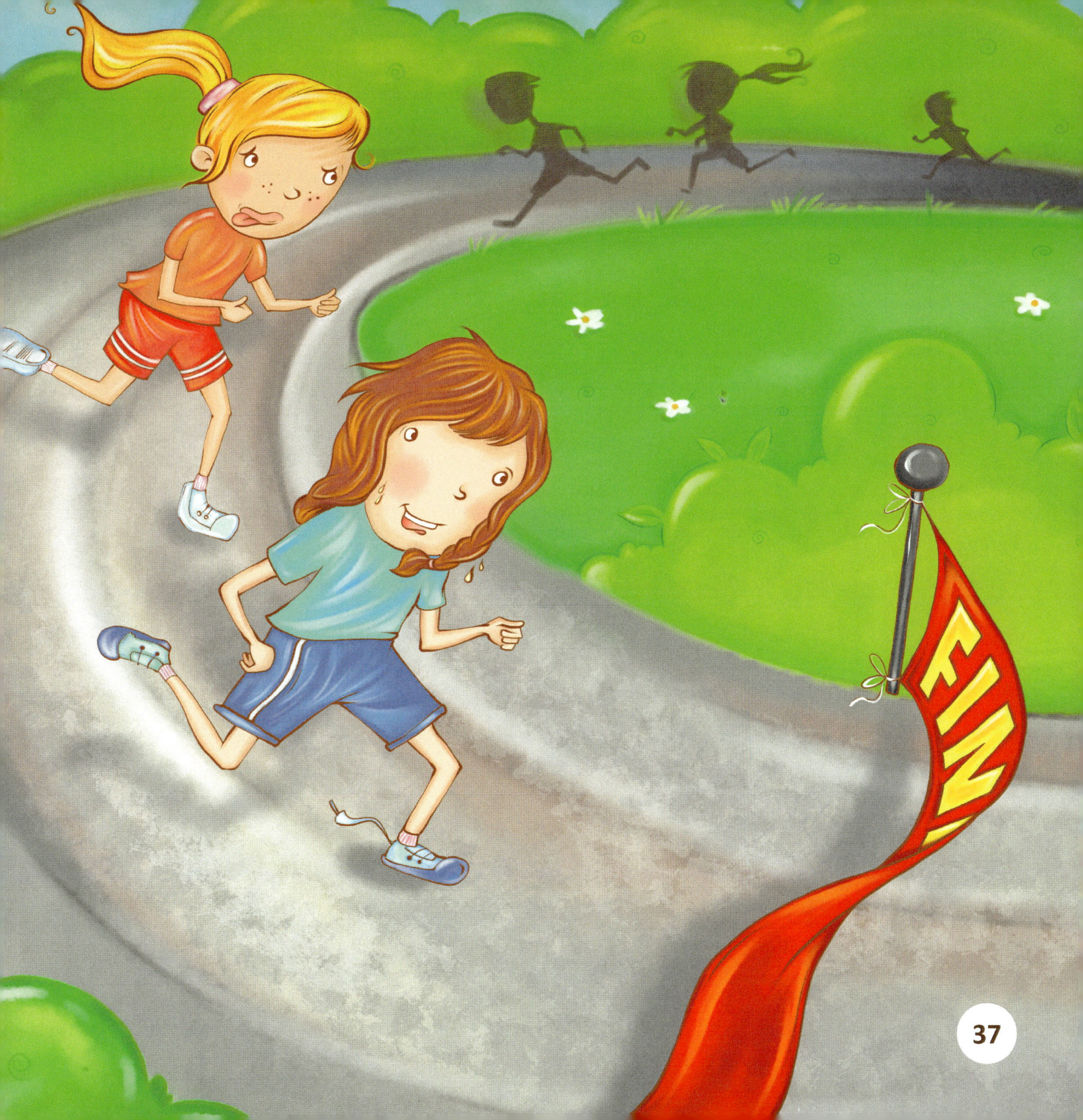
FIN

She crosses the finish line in second place, scoring five points for her team. She smiles as she reaches for her water bottle, breathing in and out to control her breathing.

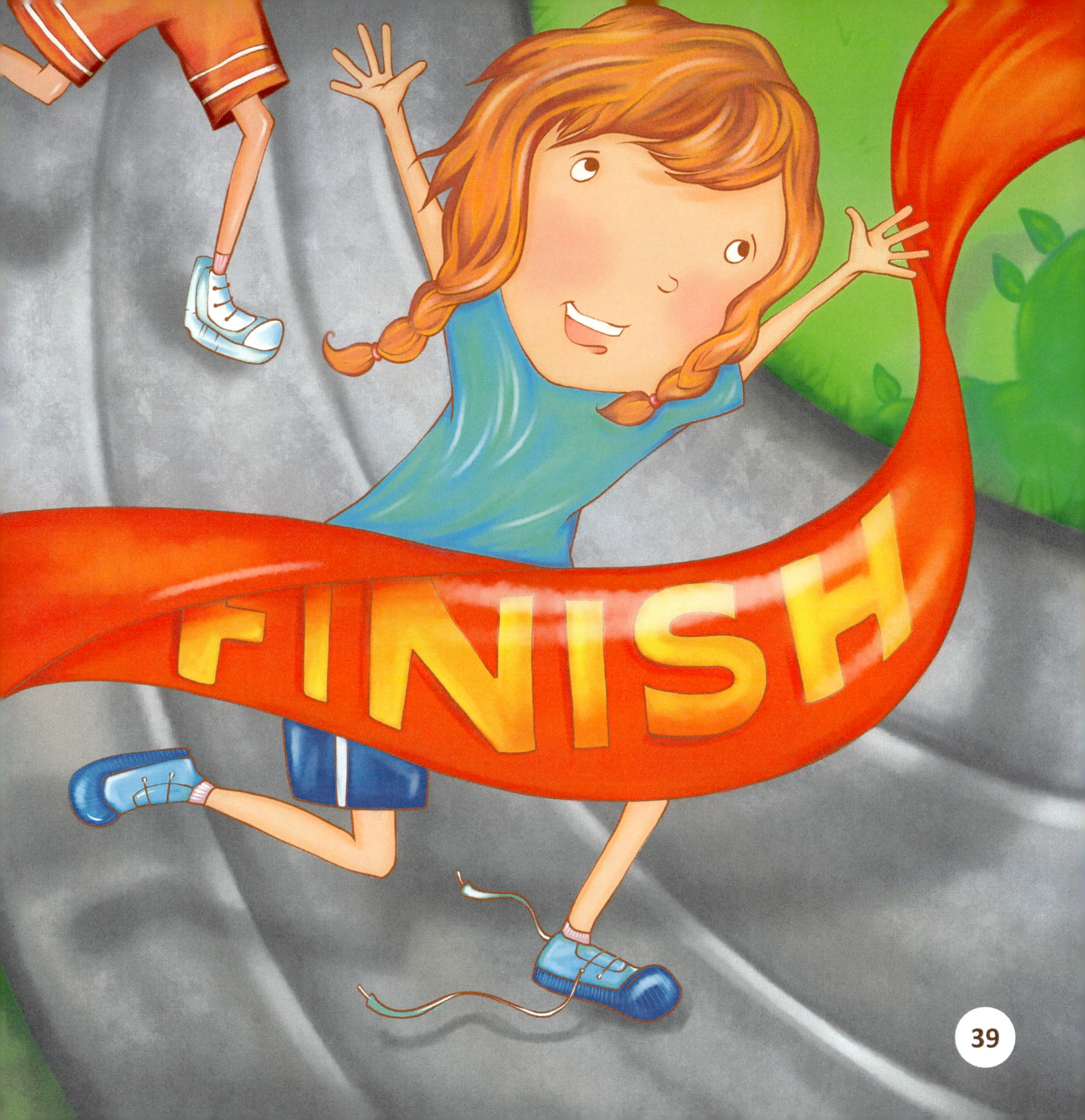
FINISH

Bending over to tie her shoelace, she winces slightly in pain and clutches her side of her stomach. You can do it. Just breathe. She won!

Laura knows she cannot let her disease hold her back or define who she is. She is not her illness, and she can do anything if she sets her mind to it.

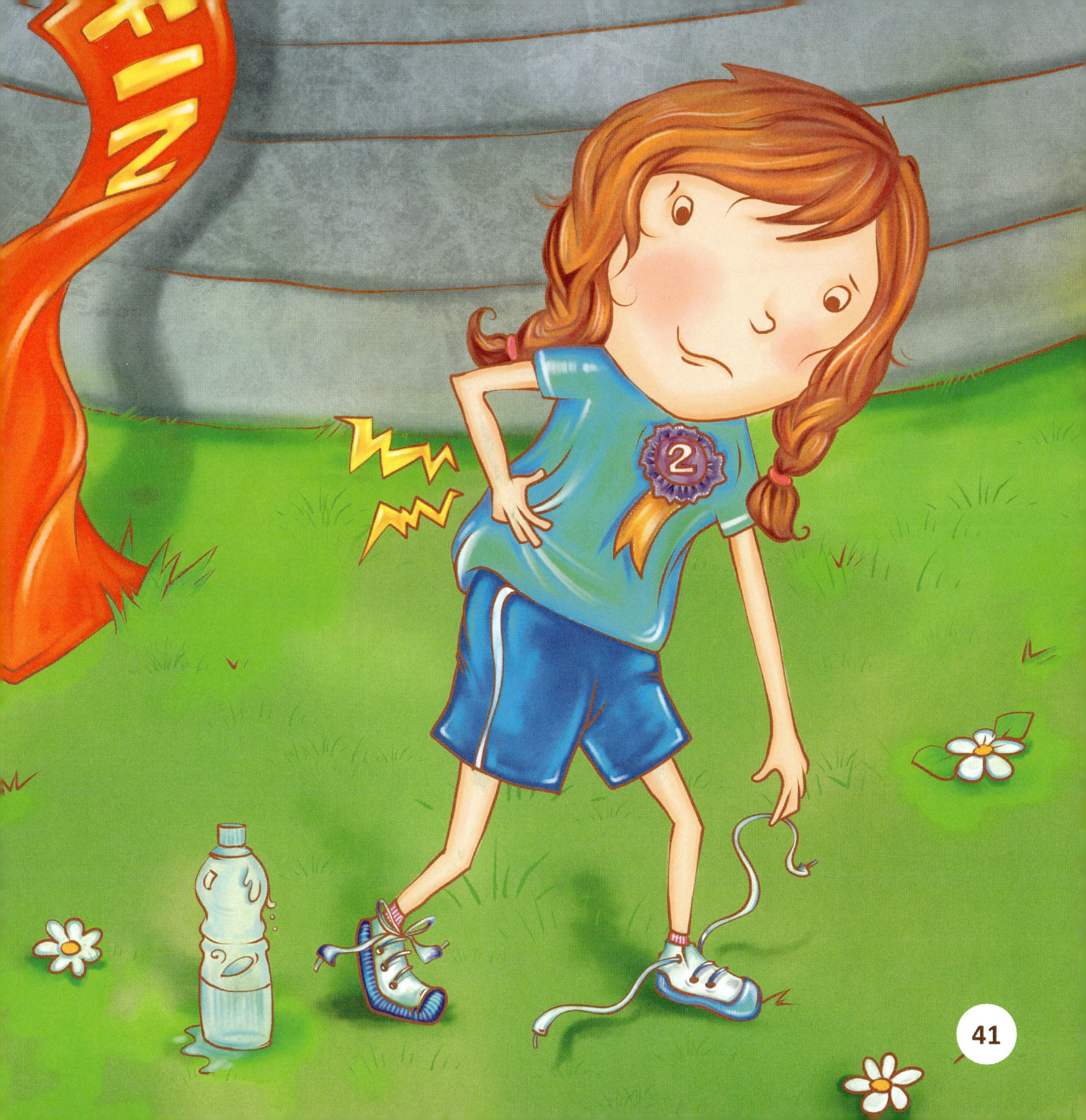
FIN
2

After the races are over, Laura and her classmates file back into the classroom. The teacher tells them to pick a partner and find a space for their butterflies to grow in the classroom.

Laura and Sami choose each other as partners. They set up their space and wait for the butterflies.

43

"You know, I just realized something. You're like a butterfly. You keep going and keep flying, never stopping to give up," Sami says.

Laura smiles. "Yeah, I guess," she says.

45

If every time she didn't feel good she stayed in bed, she'd never do anything. She's learned to adjust and change her life to make it work. Her normal isn't anybody else's normal, she thinks, but it lets her be the one to live her life.

Laura smiles even wider. She's going to be just fine.